In the Easiest Words

Poems about Love, Relationships, and Break-ups

Emma Eiler

Chaos Hatter Publishing

I dedicate this book to everyone who has been in a toxic, abusive, or bad relationship. My heart goes out to you and know that you are more important then they would like you to believe.

Contents

A Letter To You
Dear Reader

Dear Reader,

Thank you for picking up this book of Poems. These poems were written when I was in relationships, dealing with break-ups, and having a crush on someone who never took their shot until it was to late. I hope that you will be able to relate to them. These poems helped me to understand my feelings at the time and I hope that as you read them that you are able to understand yours and be able to get the closer that you need. I am sorry if you have experienced some of the same types of situations that I was in and I hope that I am able to help you recognize it. You do not deserve to be treated bad by anyone especially by the one that says that they love you. You are worth more then that do not let others tell you are worthless. With out further of ado turn the page to read the poems.

Love,

Emma

Gaslight

Take a breath
Take a hit
Take a shot
But remember this

You are wonderful
You are beautiful
You are amazing
But remember this

Those thoughts
Inside your head
Will keep you down
Will keep you from believing
Will keep you from succeeding

Your own worst enemy
Is the voice inside your head
Keeping you locked
Inside a cage of glass
Wishing you were dead

As cold and alone
As you feel
Is nothing
But
The wounded voice
Inside your head

All Because of you

Tears rolling down my cheeks
As I sat there saying no
How could you do that
My heart will never be the same

Ignored by everyone
Good and bad
Thrown away like a broken record
Never to see the light again

I hear the sound of rolling thunder
Then in your stone cold eyes
I see the lightening flash
And then coldness starts to take over

The sadness dwells inside
The person one knows is now lost
In a pond of sadness
Brought on by you

You hold the forbidden fruit

You hold all evil
Your eyes bring shame
Your smile brings evil

Hearing the rain go pitter patter
On the small square window
Staring in the dark room
Of the house

Seeing in the middle
A cold alone chair
And there sits the person
Who I used to know

Bound in chains of gold
There it sits
It's passed out
And it will never see
The sun shine again

All because of what you did
You brought all evil
And now your escaping
Because you were the one
Who put it there

Going through girls
One by one
Breaking all their hearts
Seeing no lights

But the evil still consumes you
The world is now different
The evil now consumes it
And it's all because of you

You try to escape it
Trying to shake it off
Trying to run away
When innocent people
Get hurt

All because of you!

Gone

By the time you are done reading this
I will be gone
You will come to follow me
Yet never find me

For what I am writing
Is the truth of it
And no longer will the truth ever haunt me
My feelings will be left
For everyone to see
And you will see the true love I held

But you never saw it
I kept it hidden for all those years
I look down at the blood
Which has pooled at my feet
For I have taken out
The very thing that pains me
I no longer have a heart
With that said
I will die never knowing true love
All because I pulled my heart out

To try and mend it
Because of you

Am I hard to love?
I just wish I could know
What makes me so easy to
Walk away from
To make people stop loving me
I am sick and tired of people leaving
Every footstep
Every last word
Every lets be friends
Kills my heart a little more
I just want to be numb
Feel nothing at all
Make this pain go away
So that I can
Just be free
Away from you
Into the great unknown
Lost
But
Finally
Unharmed
I want to know Love

Love
That four letter word
Holds so much weight
Has started so many wars
I think that is all humans want
Is to be loved
But the other side
The selfish side
Wont let us be
Wont make it that simple
To just love me.

Beauty on the Inside

How can people love someone
So much and yet
Not even know them

Because a lot of people
Love with their eyes
And not with their hearts

Are you one of them?
Because if you are
I don't want you anymore

For once the beauty wears off
Or fades away
What is left of that love

Nothing
You never knew the person
Behind the beauty
On their outside

What truly matters
Or what should matter
Is what is on the inside

But to many people
Learn this to late
They hurt the ones
Who loved them the most

Because the outside
Wasn't as pretty
As their minds beauty

Remember
An Apple can be perfect on the outside
But rotten inside

And
An apple that is all beaten on the outside
can be perfect within

Beauty can be only skin deep
So when you make that choice
Make sure you love the person within

Who said you could walk
Into my life
And say that
I'm not doing it right

You say I don't know how to live
And that I live safe
I don't do anything crazy
Look at my family

I've broken a lot of hearts
Broken a lot of rules
Showed the strings
Pulled them one to many times

But I guess that
Was not good enough
And you left me empty handed
And I left you empty hearted

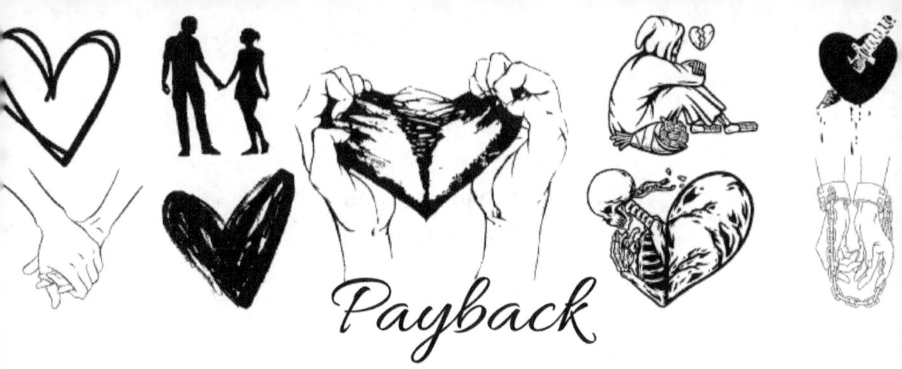

Everyday is cold
The clouds always hide the sun
There is blood stained snow
Beneath my feet

As you hang upon
That hook
Your life slowly slipping away
As I stand here watching

That cold smile crosses my face
Your eyes asking me why
My eyes ask the same
As I stare straight into your eyes

And down into your very being
Realizing all your secrets
Still not finding the one answer
To the question I want to know

Not finding it
I mount my steed

And ask out loud one more time
The question

But still there is no answer
I leave throwing the necklace
That I use to hold so dear
But now it means nothing

As I turn
You breath your last breath
And that cold smile fades

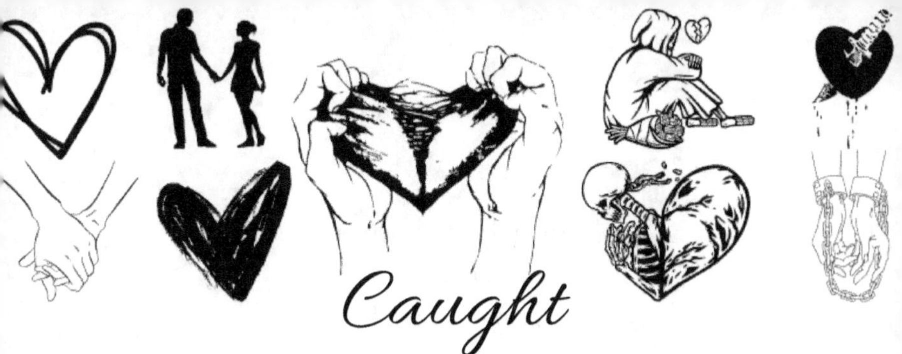

Caught

One step closer
To the edge
Wanting to jump
Without a care in the world
But then
You grab my hand
And pull me away
And into your arms
Your smell consumes me
Enclosing me
A cage that I never wanted
To leave

You bend to kiss me
And your lips taste
As good as ice cream
On a hot summer's day

Those eyes
That I love to look into
Remind me of water
And that calms me

I snuggle a little closer
Just wanting to be
As close as I can be
You feel normal to me
And my mind doesn't focus
On the number of months
I have been with you
Me being with you just feels so natural
And I love that
And I love you
And I always will

Ruled By My Heart

The acid burns my skin
And yet it heals my heart

I kick, I scream, I try to get away
But my heart wants to stay

I run away as fast as I can
But I'm standing in the same spot

My mind is telling me to go
But my heart wants me to stay

So, part of me runs like everyone else
Another part stays ruled by my heart

My mind is in a fascade
My heart is sneaky

I sit down listening to my heart
My mind is in a soundproof room

He appears out of the dust
The perfect guy just like my heart said

No Longer

No longer will I fight for you
No longer will you see
The tears that fall from my eyes
You seem to no longer care
You turn a blind eye

My hand grows cold
Without you here
My sun went away
And my happiness too
You took everything with you

Nobody needs my help
And it seems nobody wants me around
So I go to the place
That I call home
I lock myself up in there

I wait for my prince charming
But I don't believe in fairy tales
So, he will never come
Do you believe what you see

When you look at me

Through the little window
You look at me
Expecting me to perform
But you left me
Everyone left me
To fend for myself

Breaking Up

Everyday is hell
But each day it gets better
I start to believe
You are not for me

You are my drug
Don't give me another hit
My heart may not be able to take it
And my head is not aware

Don't do this if you don't care
To hard to turn away
I'm begging for you
Wanting to get another hit

You are my drug
Don't give me another hit
My heart may not be able to take it
And my head is not aware

And then
As if the time had stopped

I found out that it is not you
That I long for

You are my drug
Don't give me another hit
My heart may not be able to take it
And my head is not aware

It is how you make me feel
Wrapped up in your arms
The Safety
But you never were safe

You are my drug
Don't give me another hit
My heart may not be able to take it
And my head is not aware

So I walk away
Shaking from withdrawals
Finally healing myself
Realizing you were my drug
And that I can live
Fine without you.

Time

Time is ticking away
Life is not how it used to be
Everything spinning around my head
Hold me Close
Don't let me loose my head

Cause I'm coming apart at the seams
Hold me tighter then before
Whisper nice words into my ears
And never look through my door

I used to be happy to see you
But I'm not
I felt the warmth of your heart
But I don't
I once welcomed you with opened arms
But they're closed

Cause I'm coming apart at the seams
Hold me tighter then before
Whisper nice words into my ears
And never look through my door

That was all before
You opened my door
And I saw the look on your face change
From love to hate
It will never be the same again

Cause I am coming apart at the seams
Hold me tighter then before
Whisper nice words into my ears
And never look through my door

Why did you have to do that
Release the monsters
For so long I kept behind that locked door
Like Pandora you had to open it
And release the bad out into the world.
Now I will forever be changed
And you should be afraid.

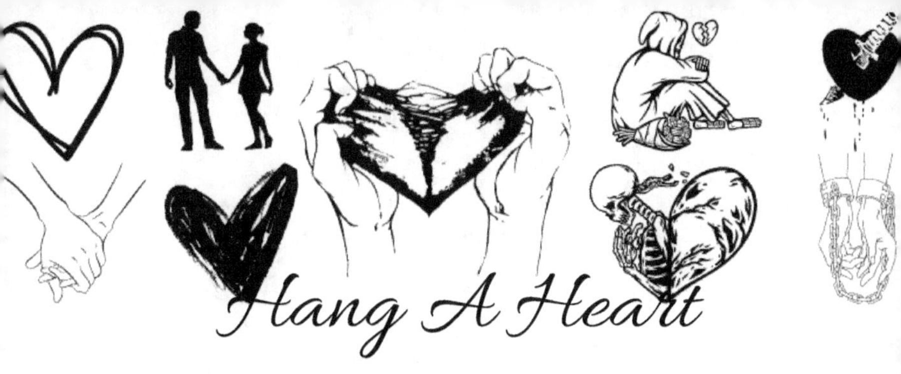

Hang A Heart

Pull a hanger out
And put my heart on it
Because you ripped it out
And took it from me

How many girls have you
Done this to
I cant be the only one
But if you say so
Then I must be

When you decide you don't want it
And you are going to throw it out
Tell me I will come and get it
When you don't need it
To get your kicks from

I gave it to you
Hoping you would treat it nice
But you took it as a prize
And never planned to give it back
But you see it is yours

I don't care about it anymore
I don't need a heart to live
I am invisible to all who walk
No one sees the pain
No one wants to and no one cares either

You turned away
The day was cold
I looked after you
Longing to grab your hand
But by the time I reached out
You were to far gone

I won't call your name
Wait up for you
Keep the light on all night
I'll find my own way
Look up to find you are gone
And not miss that sad face
You are hiding there

I deleted your number
So, I won't think of you
But it is a lie
Cause I always do
I throw the picture away
And don't think of you

I won't call your name
Wait up for you
Keep the light on all night
I'll find my own way
Look up to find you are gone
And not miss that sad face
You are hiding there
Because I am done.

Pull that rope a little more

To hold me up and away from the pit

It is filled with the hurt of these lies

Then

You

Let

Go

And I fall

And I brake

I fall into the pit of lies

Consumed now with that very thing

I fall through the bottom

And into hell

My body slumps against a wall

Not able to move

There

Is

A

Pain

In

My

Hands

I

Feel

A

Pull

My arms begin to rise

My feet begin to move

My eyes look up

To see who is doing this

There you stand

The puppet master

Controlling my string

Then you are gone

When the lights come up

I

turn

And

whirl

As you tell me too

The lights blind me

I obey silently

The show is over

The puppet master makes me bow

The lights go down

I hear the clapping

And see smiling faces

Then I realize

These people are

My friends and family

They were watching me

All along

How will you ever know
The feelings that I hold
I see you staring
And when I look at you
You smile and laugh
Which makes me laugh
And makes me smile
Even in the times I don't want to
I am happy when we are together
And I think of you when we are not
Every night I wish
For you to ask that question
But you haven't yet
But I'll be patient
Waiting
Hoping
Praying
For that day to come
But the thing is
I won't wait forever

Don't

Don't tell me how to be
Don't hit me that way
Don't smile when you say no
Don't try to be a hero
Don't try to be everything to me
Don't laugh when I get hurt
Don't try to understand
Don't yell when I am wrong
Don't lie to me
You say you love me then
Don't try to change me
Don't understand me
Just love me for me

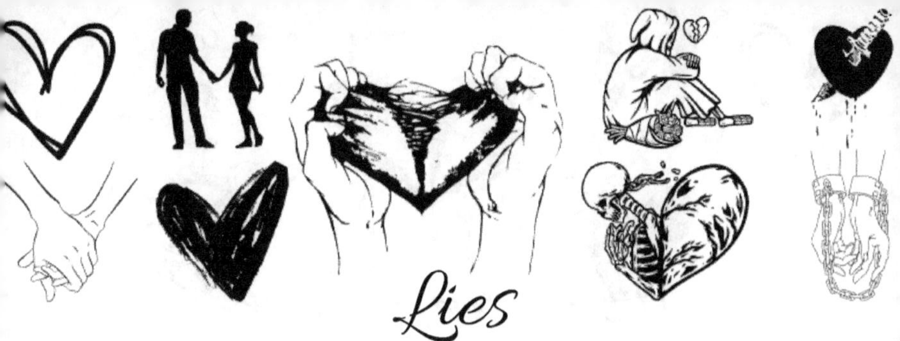

Your eyes are like poison
And your words untruthful
All your lies make me
Go insane
I swear
If I hear one more
I will go crazy
But then again
I see your smile
And I know
You won't stop lying
Even if your life depends on it
And I don't ever see
Our life advancing
So I just smile
And let it play out

Hide and Seek

My eyes are closed
I'm counting the time
I'm playing a game
I'm hiding my face

I wonder who the next will be
To find and hold me
I realize who I want
Will never be the one I need

I see a face
They come into my world
Never staying for very long
I hold my head and cry
Though nothing will be alright

I can't wait for one person
To come and say I love you
But I've been waiting my whole life
And still they have not come

So I sit here waiting

Huddled in a corner
Away from the world
Of hatred and misery

Stop!

I tell myself to stop
But I can't stop
I try to tell you things
But you just won't listen
I have said these things
Over and over again
But it always seems like
It's the first time you heard it
I scream out for your attention
But you turn the other way
You hold me back against my will
That's when I get mad at you
You never hold me tight
And say everything will be alright
I feel as if I'm ready to scream
But no sound comes out
And you wonder why
I like to get out
Stop fooling around Babe
When you say
Your the one that keeps me sane
HA, that's funny babe

Well I don't know aint it
The words you say hurts my ears
And stings my mind
Because they're all lies
But I don't let those get to me
You try to comfort me
But you don't even know
How that is not true love!

Guardian Angel

You touch my hand

I freeze

Not knowing what to do

Each time I see you smile

I just want to melt

But I would never show you

Maybe it won't happen

The next time I see you

But it always does

It doesn't matter

How much I say I'm over you

Because each time you come around

It happens all over again

Nothing helps take the pain away

It is like pouring salt

Into my wounds

The burning

It kills

But it soothes the voices

That cries out

And every second of the day

It seems so hard to take

I need you out of here
With each pounding step you take
I call for you
Cry for you
But you don't notice
I'm invisible to you
And I will always be won't I
I'm your guardian angel
Always by your side
But always watching quietly

The wind blowing my hair
Knowing you are right there
Always holding my hand
Never to let go again

Standing on a cliff
Looking down and seeing the ground
Knowing it is so far away
Knowing I may fall

Not knowing what death brings
Not knowing what the future brings
If you are there or not
The simple beat of your heart

But at the same time
I hate all that too
Expect for one thing
And that is

I could never hate you!

Tiny Dancer

You sat there
Watching me
As if I were your tiny dancer
But that would mean that
You care for me
In which you don't
For you wouldn't even notice
If I were gone
You just sit on the throne
Looking down on your kingdom
Well fuck that
I will not be a part of that
I have my own life to live
So I leave
Getting out of those stupid clothes
That you made me wear
And like a puppet
I do
I walk out of your world
And into a pure white one
I start to imagine
The scene hops upon my walls

Soon "your people" come to me
Then you come here too
And ask to be here
I reply with a no
You walk away slowly
Not knowing what to do
For those people never loved you
They were there to see me
Your tiny Dancer
And now that I am gone
They are too
And let me tell you this
I will never go back to you
and be the tiny dancer.

How Can I Tell You This

The fighting won't stop
And the pain is way to much
And I keep getting these marks
No one will approach me
My fading has just begun
I want to hide my face
As I sit here and cry
But can the people not see
That they were the ones
That put these scars on me
I didnt want them too
But they hurt me to bad
The world around me keeps spinning
And in my head I wonder who I am
How can no one see the pain that they cause
When it seems to go on forever
The time will last forever
The rain now begins to pour
Down on the ones with hurt
Stinging the wounds from the past
And I can not stay

I hardly know what to say
And then I see you
My hurting stops
The pain is gone
I begin to have fun
I forget the past
I start to really look towards the future
Because I love you so much
Then you will ever know

I am Fine

I was in your arms
We were happy as could be

But then I was taken away
And I saw the sadness on your face

You wept
But no tears fell

You were sad
But you did not frown

Whether or not you truly were
Only you will know

You turned away to quick
Just as I needed your help

I tried to get your attention
But you wasted it all on another girl

She had long blonde hair

She was pretty as could be

I was cast out into the shadows
When some guy came

And picked me up
He carried me out of the shadows

And when you saw me with him you flipped
Realizing the mistake you made

But now I'm in love with him
Come to think about it

I never really liked you

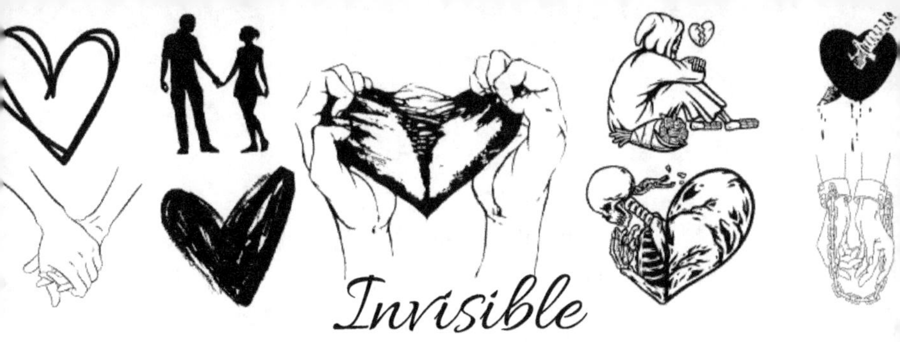

Invisible

My heart was beating
As he walked by
The realization of reality came
But it seemed as though
I was maybe invisible
To him about the way I feel
It seemed I was always in
A daydream dancing for
The one I called king
But then the dream is over
And I am back to my life
Not wanting to go home
If I ever had a place like that
My heart goes on pounding
With every step I take
The willingness to live
Is now coming to an almost end
But the realization of life
Puts its hand on me
And I realize I can't die
I need to go on
People pass by

I try to hold on
But I always seem to slip
People seem not to notice
I miss the family I used to have
Look at yourselves
I try to run
But I can't move
My feet won't go anywhere
I walk through life
With a fake smile upon my face
Just to throw you off my trail
But I realize I could never
Because you love me to much
I can't tell you I don't love you
Because that would be a lie
And I would do anything for you

I try to tell myself
That this is all pretend
That the room is not spinning
And I'm not this way

But I can not pretend any longer
This brick wall is getting to high
Filled with all these lies
I ever told

I can't believe the way you look
I can't believe you stare
I'm walking back and forth
Trying to get your glare
Away from me

I see how we used to be
You only see how we are now
You push away the good times we had
And I pull them near
For that is what I really need right now

I don't want your arms around me
That were once so loving
But they're now the things I dread
Don't even touch me
Keep your hands off

You can't see what's right in front of you
Can't you see that
I don't love you
And we're done

Keep the wheels turning
On that old car
And leaving me
All alone in a world unlike my own
And to think that I loved you
All along and then
You say you don't
That you were just playing
Around to make someone Jealous

You are a loven jerk
That's me being nice
I don't ever want to see
Your loven face around here anymore

But now I'm just getting mad
And for what
So some jerk gets pleasure
And don't "oh honey" me
Because I'm sick and tired
Of your loven face
And

Don't you dare call me honey again

The Time

Remember the times
When I was happy
And you were too
Remember the times

Listen to the times
When you were happy
And I was sad
Listen to the times

Relive the times
When I spoke no words
And you were always mad
Relive the times

Play the movie back
When I was happy
And you were very sad
Play the movie back

I remember all these times
And relive each one

And in time I will forget them
And I will forget you!

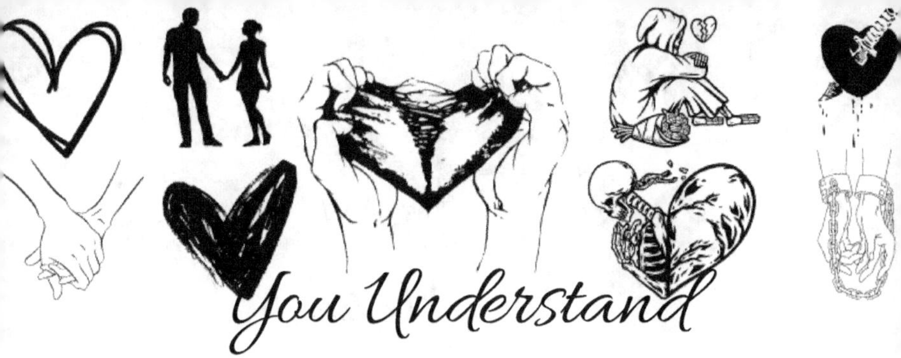

You Understand

I look into your eyes
And you look into mine
And there is something that tells me
That everything is going to be fine
And that I'm not alone
Even in the times of my greatest pain
You are there
Out of all the people I expected
To be there it was you
Every time I would have a problem
You always seemed to give me advise
To keep going to never give up
I guess in those talks we had
I learned you knew what I was going through
That is when I knew it was true
The feelings for me and you

No More Waiting

I don't know what to say
You have changed way to much
I don't even know the real you
You stare at me
But I no longer stare back
I feel as if I'm in the dark
I know they're your friends too
But that doesn't mean I am a secondary one
I won't always be there
If you just toss me a side
I won't be waiting there
Like a rag doll
But whatever do what you want
But you might not find me at the end

Things Never Said

The dream

The nightmare

The life I live

The steps

The time

The empty space

The letter

The word

The note I wrote

To you

To me

But you never read

So you didn't stay

The love

The Hate

The feelings no one knows

The secrets

The lies

The late nights

But now

I am gone

The walls are closing in
I think I'm going crazy
The ceilings coming down
Now I am really gone
The room is closing in
And now I see a figure
The lights start to flicker
And now its getting closer
There is one more lasting moment of light
And now I see your face
And now the room is dark
I see a spot of light
These are the last seconds
It's getting bigger
My last breath
It consumes me
And the last thing I saw was
You

Stories You Tell

You think you know everything
When you really know nothing
Just sittin right there talking shit
Thinking your fooling everyone
Well I got news for you
You're not fooling anyone
You make up stories left and right
Not really thinking of who you're hurting
But I got news for you
You have hurt everyone in your life
And that is why
At the end of the day there is no one there
For you
All because the stories you tell
And the victim role you play

I close my eyes
You take a step
I feel the world draw back in fear
You take another
I start to feel scared

Another step
Another wasted moment
Another word
Another waste of time
Another lie
Another waste of breath

I can't take this anymore

Close your eyes
As I do
Whisper slowly
As you do
Hold me close
As others do

And don't waste my time on you

Your Real Feelings

So what you love me
Bet you can't see who I truly am
By one look in my eyes
Or what are you to afraid
That one look into my eyes
And you won't love me

But you see you forgot one thing
And that is that time will truly tell
And whether I love you or not
Time will tell everything

So put your feelings on the table
And take the time to care
If your just playing a game
Well then just play it
But you won't win because
I would never go out with you

So take the time to consider
What you truly feel
And leave the others in the dust

Don't listen to what they say
Because they don't know your feelings
And reach into your mind
And pull out your feelings

How can you just sit there
Looking at this with amazement
With wide eyes and an open jaw
The words not coming out

Until someone calls freeze
And time itself stops
You sitting there with that look upon your face
And me untouched by time

As the whole world freezes
And me alone not frozen
Forever in the shadows
Of the lies that forever put me there

The empty promises fill my brain
With the thought of happiness
Of us together forever
But that is all gone
Lost in the freezing darkness
Of time.

The Place I Want to Be

The fire blazes
It is a nice pretty blaze
That you could roast marshmallow too
I love the way it lights your face
Your arms around me
Brings more comfort

The music
A nice background
To set the mood
And I get up to dance
You watch
Eyes never leaving me
Good thing it's just you and me

The forest is quiet
Like it always is
But it's just for us
I love you
But you already know that

But then I wake up
I realized that it was just a dream
That makes me sad
Cause I want to be there
Just us
Cause I love you

If That's Okay

My hand touches the flame
But it doesn't burn me
It comforts me
In ways I never knew things could
But then again
You were the one person
That I thought would

But you didn't
After you promised
Me, you would never leave
But I realized
You are just not that into me
And you know what
That is perfectly fine with me

Cause one thing with me loving you
Is that I want you to be happy
And if I am not the person
You are happy with
That is fine
Because I have always

EMMA EILER

Put my feelings second
In everything
But one thing
Don't think I will always be there
Cause I am going to go live my life
If that's okay

The Hardest Words to Say

Why can I write these words
To you so easily
Yet saying them
Takes more courage
Then I have in my body

I can never say it first
You say it first
And I say it back
But every time
I go to say it
It gets trapped

Do I really love you
The answer is yes
For I have thought
To long and can only
Find that I do
I can't live another
Moment without you

My heart yearns for and
I'm pretty sure it beats
For you
My arms fit comfortably
Around you
And your always on my mind

The Jump

That jump
Could have killed me
But it didn't
Because it made me forget
You
Which makes me thankful
Because thoughts of you
Would have been the death of me

We were not suppose to be together
But you said we would
And I believed
That stupid lie
And you said it so many times
Yet you left
Just like you said you wouldn't
Stupid me

Another thing you promised
But broke
I am not another one of those girls
I realized what you do

Promising me, telling me
Exactly what I want to hear
But did you ever think twice
Of what you said
I guess not!

Untamable

You never claimed
You could fly
So I let you go
And you flew away
Bringing me to my knees
Tears staining my pale cheeks

But I let you go
Because I didn't know a thing
And it tore up my heart
To do it
But no longer do these chains
Hold me down

I am free
I am crazy
I am wild
But most of all
I am untamable
And I sure fooled you

You thought you held me down

But little did you know
I let you hold me down
I could have
Got away from you
But I let you catch me
Like I always do

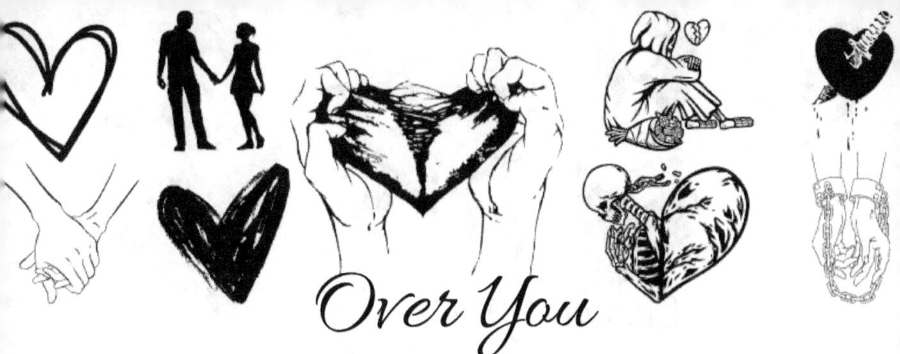

Over You

The empty seat
That wasted space
The air around you
Those wasted tears
Why did I cry for you
Why did I love you
Did you even love me
Like you said
Was it hard for you to utter those words
Or were they easy
Just like all the other lies
You told
And claimed that they were true
Do you tell every girl these lies
Or just me
You know what
I don't even want to know
There is just one thing
I wish you the worst
And another
I hope you miss me
Like I miss you

Changing Your Ways

You use to always be there
And we had some fun times
But then your addiction took over
And now you never call
Or come over
The only time we talk is
On the computer
And that is not a lot
I don't know what to tell you
Or even what to say to you
But hey whatever
When you need me
I might not be there
And when you want to ask that question
I might not be free
And then you will know
You missed your chance
Of ever being with me
Because of the stupid addiction
Took over
So blame yourself

Not Your Toy

The doorbell rings
But I don't want to answer
Knowing it is you
The person I don't want to talk to
You were the one to make
The decision and not get
Any closer to me
Or just to hang out
I will always be there for you
But where will those games
Be to bail you out
When times get rough
One day you will want to hang out
And I will say no
Or I will not be there for you
And that day is today
Maybe tomorrow maybe we will see
But most likely no
I'm not someone you can call on
Whenever you want to
So I won't answer because I'm
Not a toy I'm a

Human!

Turn Your Cheek

I wake up with tears in my eyes
It's the same thing I did last night
My breath is getting shorter
I look upon my bed
As if expecting you to be there

But you're not
And that pains me
More then the deepest cut
I go outside
And start to play a game
When I realize your never coming out

Every time the phone rings
I expect it to be you
But it is not
I love the way you make me laugh
And never make me cry

I love when we're together
I hate when we're apart
You will never know the feelings that I hold

I sit by you
And see your hand
I just want to hold it

But the thing is I can't
I think of you every night
I wonder why we aren't
Sitting together
Watching the waves go by

Calling Your Name

How many times do you have
To call someones name so they will stop
Because I keep calling your name
And you never stop and wait

All these times I stopped and waited for you
What were they for
They were for nothing
Absolutely nothing

Now that I take the time to slow
I slow myself down to a stop
And I stop and I wait
Because I thought I heard my name

But the again these hallways are becoming dark
And I don't know who is speaking
I try not to listen to everyones yelling
And my heart skips a few beats

There are voices all around me

Some I don't even know
But yours is a high clear voice
I hear above the rest

Meant To Be

I think of you
Every day
We are meant to be
We are so much a like
We could never get in a fight
I just want you
To hold me tight
I think of you
Always
Your never not on my mind
However
We are not together
And never have we been
But that doesn't mean
My heart doesn't ache for you
A story
That has never been written
In time
And
I guess I will
Have to be fine
With that

Be My Hero

Don't be my hero
Be the bad guy
Be the one to make me cry
Because evil is so much better

I don't want a guy with an even temper
Or doesn't break the rules
Cause what's the fun in that

At least that is what I thought
I have been with them
And I don't want that anymore

I want a nice guy
Someone I feel safe with
Held tight in their arms
Who is supportive
And Kind
And caring

But where
Do those guys hide

I feel like
I am searching
In the dark

Unable to find
My way to him
Away from the bad
And into the arms
Of the good

One Step At a Time

I walked
Upon that day
The cold wind
Biting at my face
Hardly knowing
What was going on
Taking one step
At a time
Thoughts running
Through my mind

This is the day
My whole life
Crumbled to pieces
The day you first
Hit me
Nothing was ever that same
Your arms
No longer secure
In fact
They were the things

I feared the most

But one hit
Was not enough
For you
It continued
Until the end
Of the relationship
So I ran away from you
And I will continue too

www.ingramcontent.com/pod-product-compliance
Lightning Source LLC
Chambersburg PA
CBHW051133160726
47997CB00019B/2349